DARK HEARTS

THE WORLD'S MOST FAMOUS HORROR WRITERS

W

PENGUIN WORKSHOP
An Imprint of Penguin Random House LLC, New York

Penguin supports copyright. Copyright fuels creativity, encourages
diverse voices, promotes free speech, and creates a vibrant culture.
Thank you for buying an authorized edition of this book and for complying
with copyright laws by not reproducing, scanning, or distributing any part of
it in any form without permission. You are supporting writers and allowing
Penguin to continue to publish books for every reader.

Text copyright © 2021 by Penguin Random House LLC.
Illustrations copyright © 2021 by Karl James Mountford. All rights reserved.
Published by Penguin Workshop, an imprint of Penguin Random House LLC,
New York. PENGUIN and PENGUIN WORKSHOP are trademarks of
Penguin Books Ltd, and the W colophon is a registered trademark of
Penguin Random House LLC. Manufactured in China.

Visit us online at www.penguinrandomhouse.com.

Library of Congress Control Number: 2021026615

ISBN 9780593222782   10 9 8 7 6 5 4 3 2 1 TOPL

DARK HEARTS

THE WORLD'S MOST FAMOUS HORROR WRITERS

BY JIM GIGLIOTTI

ILLUSTRATED BY KARL JAMES MOUNTFORD

PENGUIN WORKSHOP

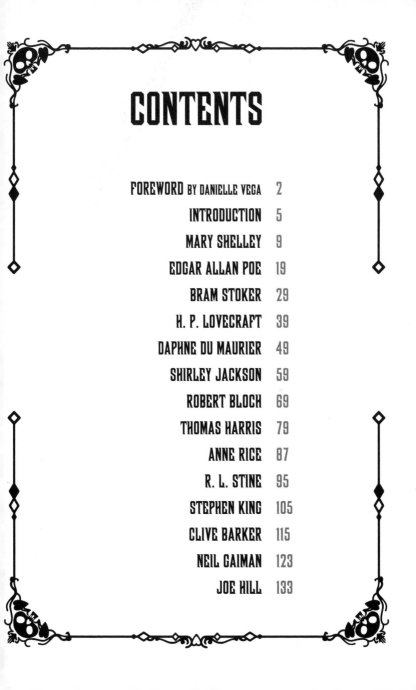

CONTENTS

FOREWORD

DANIELLE VEGA

Picture this: a campfire in the deep woods, leaping flames, crackling logs and, just beyond, the perfect dark of night. Now, this is where you're going to have to use your imagination, because this isn't the kind of dark that you and I are used to. It's the dark of a world before electric lights and skyscrapers, before interstates and the internet. It's uninterrupted, velvet black. The kind of darkness that could—and often *did*—hide absolutely anything.

This is where the first scary stories were told. People gathered around those fires to tell stories about what would happen if you journeyed beyond the safety of your village or tribe, if you tempted fate, or if you got lost in the woods. I'm always skeptical when someone tells me they aren't a fan of horror, because I believe that telling scary stories is part of what makes us human, same as the ability to use tools, empathize with others, or imagine the future. Scary stories tell us where the boundaries are, they make sense of our fears, and they teach us how to be brave. Scary stories were some of the first stories human beings ever told.

Maybe it's no surprise that I was raised on a steady diet of horror. I know every author profiled in this book so well that they feel like some of my oldest and dearest friends. Stephen King wrote my earliest bedtime stories—or he might as well have; my mother made up stories based on his novels long before I could read his books myself. In college, I learned that when she was my age, Mary Shelley invented the horror genre when the idea for a novel about a reanimated man came to her in a dream. As an adult learning to write horror stories of my own, I devoured anything I could find by Shirley Jackson, reveling in the way she was able to make even the most mundane things (a cat! a teapot! a bowl of sugar!) absolutely menacing. And just a couple of years ago, while making my way to a panel at Comic-Con to discuss my own horror novels, I walked past Joe Hill. I had one hand up, all set to wave and say, "Hey, Joe," before I remembered that I only know him from his books, not real life.

If this is your first time learning about any of the authors profiled in the pages of this book, I can say that I am truly and deeply jealous. They will scare you, yes, but they will also challenge you, entertain you, make you laugh, and make you think. People will tell you to read scary stories with the lights on, but in my experience, the light just makes the darkness beyond seem even darker. Who knows what it might be hiding?

INTRODUCTION

What are you scared of? Public speaking? Spiders? The dark?

Those are very real fears, and there are plenty of others. Some are serious, like the fear of being alone (autophobia) or the fear of confined spaces (claustrophobia). Some seem less so—like the fear of clocks (chronomentrophobia) or the fear of the number thirteen (triskaidekaphobia).

We all have our fears. So why would we want to pick up a scary book and frighten ourselves even more?

Maybe it's because we know we can always close the book if things get too intense. Or maybe it's because reading horror gives us a way to confront our fears. Perhaps if we read how Neil Gaiman's seven-year-old protagonist in *The Ocean at the End of the Lane* stands up to his evil nanny, then getting up and speaking in front of a classroom won't feel so daunting. Maybe if we read how Clive Barker's ten-year-old hero, Harvey, gets away from the soul-sucking Mr. Hood by tricking him in *The Thief of Always*, then that spider on the windowsill doesn't seem like such a big deal.

But what about Gaiman, Barker, and the other authors who are famous for their horrific tales?

They are not free from being afraid. As a youngster, Stephen King slept with the light on for fear of the dark. Barker was afraid of flying. R. L. Stine was afraid of jumping into a swimming pool. Edgar Allan Poe and Shirley Jackson never got past some of their worst inner fears.

The fourteen authors profiled on the following pages face their fears, and ours, by drawing on a dark part of their hearts for inspiration in their writing.

They write about the horror of the natural world and the supernatural. They write of physical terror and psychological terror.

As varied as their styles and their personalities are, what all these authors have in common is that they began reading at a very early age. Many read scary stories, weird tales, horror novels, and comic books when they were young. But they also read fantasy, science fiction, and classic literature. Reading was the key that unlocked the door of their active imaginations. "We all have fevered imaginative lives," Barker says. "Otherwise, we wouldn't be doing what we are doing."

The results of their dark hearts are classics of horror literature. Some of the books and stories by these fourteen writers have been read for many decades. And many are sure to still be read a very long time from now.

MARY SHELLEY

MARY SHELLEY

"It was a dark and stormy night" is an old—and often reused—opening line. But it really was a dark and stormy night in 1816 when Mary Shelley created *Frankenstein*. More than two hundred years later, it is considered the first major horror story and is still read around the world. Even more than that, Frankenstein's monster has become one of the most famous popular-culture icons ever. The character has been portrayed often in movies, on television, and in music, comics, toys, and games, making it instantly recognizable.

Let's clear up one common misconception right

away: Frankenstein is not the name of the monster in Mary Shelley's novel, which was published in 1818 with the official title *Frankenstein; or, The Modern Prometheus*. Instead, Frankenstein is the name of the being's creator, Dr. Victor Frankenstein. In Mary's writing, Dr. Frankenstein's creation doesn't have a name. Mary most often calls it a "creature" or a "fiend." There have been many visual interpretations of the novel over the years. But actor Boris Karloff's portrayal of the monster in the 1931 movie, *Frankenstein*, is especially responsible for the image we think of today.

Mary Wollstonecraft Godwin was born in 1797 in London, England. Her father was William Godwin, a well-known writer and political philosopher. Her mother was Mary Wollstonecraft. She was a writer and philosopher, too. Wollstonecraft was an advocate of women's rights. She was a passionate feminist before that term even existed. She argued in her writing that women suffered from a lack of education. She felt they could be valuable contributors in all facets of culture if not held back by a society dominated by men.

That may sound like common sense today, but it was a radical, and controversial, idea in the late eighteenth century.

Unfortunately, Mary never knew her mother. Wollstonecraft became sick from complications during childbirth and died only eleven days after Mary was born. Godwin married a neighbor several years after Wollstonecraft's death, but Mary never got along with her.

It was Godwin, then, who primarily raised Mary. Though she had little formal schooling, she read often from her father's considerable library. Young Mary paid close attention to the many prominent thinkers who visited the family's London home. She listened in on lively discussions about the arts and sciences, philosophy, and politics.

One frequent guest in the Godwin home before Mary was born was Luigi Galvani, an Italian doctor, scientist, and philosopher. Galvani believed that the dead might be brought back to life through electrical stimulation. In an experiment in 1780, he found that he could make a dead frog's legs twitch with a jolt of electricity. That discovery came to be called "galvanism."

More than two decades after Galvani's initial frog experiments, his nephew, Giovanni Aldini, took his uncle's theories further. In 1803, Aldini conducted a public experiment in London on the corpse of a man who had been executed for murder. Aldini stimulated the corpse's face and muscles with electrical impulses. The dead man's eye fluttered open. His jaw quivered. One hand clenched, then lifted. His legs moved. It was such a scary and shocking scene that one man died of a heart attack while witnessing it!

Mary would have been too young to see Aldini's experiment, but it was a big deal in London. She likely would have heard her father discussing it with his guests.

Another of Godwin's guests was Percy Bysshe Shelley, a writer and poet five years older than Mary. Shelley fell in love with Mary. Godwin did not approve of the interest that Shelley took in his daughter because Shelley already was married, although unhappily so. But sixteen-year-old Mary had a mind of her own. In 1814, she and Shelley ran off to France along with Mary's stepsister, Claire.

After the death of Percy Shelley's first wife

in 1816, Mary and Percy married. That year, they were traveling in Switzerland with Claire and their son, William. They were staying near Lake Geneva with Lord Byron, another poet, and John Polidori, a writer and physician. But the weather in Geneva was terrible. Severe storms kept them inside. To keep themselves entertained, Lord Byron suggested they each come up with a ghost story.

For several days, Mary struggled for an idea that would "make the reader dread to look round, to curdle the blood," she later wrote. Then one night, the conversation turned to galvanism. When Mary went to bed, she imagined a creature that could come to life through electrical stimulation. "I saw the hideous phantasm of a man stretched out, and then, on the working of some powerful engine, show signs of life, and stir with an uneasy, half vital motion."

The myth of Frankenstein was born.

At first, Mary envisioned a short story. With Shelley's encouragement, she turned it into a novel. It was published anonymously in 1818, when Mary was twenty. Mary's name first appeared in a printing in 1823.

Today, we usually think of Mary's creation as slow minded, scary, and evil. That's in large part because of the movies—especially Karloff's monster in 1931. But Mary created an intelligent character that spent much of the novel sharing its thoughts, feelings, and emotions. The creature struggled to find purpose in its existence. "My person was hideous and my stature gigantic," it said. "What did this mean? Who was I? What was I? Whence did I come? What was my destination? These questions continually recurred, but I was unable to solve them."

Mary also created a character that was inherently good: "My heart was fashioned to be susceptible of love and sympathy," it says. The monster rebelled against Dr. Frankenstein and turned to murder and mayhem only after its creator rejected it.

Readers loved the novel, but many critics didn't. In some ways, the book was considered scandalous. After all, few people questioned that all life comes from God, and here was eighteen-year-old Mary Shelley imagining one man creating another. Like her parents', Mary's views were considered quite radical at that time.

After *Frankenstein* was published, Mary wrote six more novels, including a science-fiction thriller about the end of the world called *The Last Man* in 1826. She authored many short stories, several travel journals, and book reviews.

However, the rest of Mary's life was marked by tragedy. Three of her four children died in infancy, and Percy Bysshe Shelley drowned in a boating accident in 1822. After Shelley's corpse, along with two of his companions, washed up on shore, the bodies were buried in the sand. A month later, Shelley's body was dug up and burned under a pile of wood, called a funeral pyre. Strangely, Shelley's heart did not burn in the fire. It was given to Mary, who kept it, wrapped in silk, until her own death at age fifty-three in 1851.

EDGAR ALLAN POE

EDGAR ALLAN POE

In 1833, a newspaper in Baltimore, Maryland, ran a story detailing how local police had nabbed a pair of grave robbers at a nearby cemetery. The thieves had been after the teeth of the buried corpses. They wanted to sell them to dentists who made sets of false teeth for their patients.

Two years later, Edgar Allan Poe's story "Berenice" was printed in a Baltimore periodical called the *Southern Literary Messenger*. "Berenice" is a gruesome story about a man who is obsessed with his beautiful cousin's teeth. After she dies, he digs up the grave and removes her teeth. But he is in such a trance that he doesn't notice she is still alive! It was a shocking story for the time period. Edgar even admitted to his editor that he originally hesitated submitting the story because it is "far too horrible."

Scholars have suggested that the newspaper account of the grave robbers inspired Edgar, who lived in Baltimore. Edgar sometimes drew on articles he covered as a newspaper writer and magazine editor or that he had read about elsewhere. While it's true that he read a lot about murder and death, Edgar's own life experiences influenced his dark stories and poems even more. Rumors of alcohol and drug abuse have long been part of Edgar's story. But those were largely put forward by unfair stories after he died. His morbid tales most likely came from crossing paths with sickness and death many times in his relatively short life.

Starting with "Berenice," Edgar became famous for his frightening tales of Gothic horror. That is a specific type of horror story that usually takes place in dark and gloomy settings like a castle or a large house. It often includes elements of romance mixed in with the supernatural.

Edgar also created the first detective mystery with his 1841 short story "The Murders in the Rue Morgue." His 1843 short story "The Tell-Tale Heart" is a classic of psychological terror. And 1845's "The Raven" made him a national celebrity and remains one of the most famous poems ever written.

Edgar was born as Edgar Poe in Boston, Massachusetts, in 1809. His brother, William, was two years older. His sister, Rosalie, was born one year after Edgar. His parents, David Jr. and Eliza, were actors, but his father left the family when Edgar was still just a baby. Then, shortly before Edgar turned three, his mother died of tuberculosis, an infection of the lungs that was very dangerous in the nineteenth century.

After Eliza's death, Edgar was taken in by the Allan family in Richmond, Virginia. Frances Allan was kind and loving toward Edgar. Her husband, John, was a successful businessman. He provided Edgar with a good education but with little love or emotional support.

Edgar briefly attended the University of Virginia in 1826, then joined the army in 1827. His first book, a short collection of poetry, had been published the same year he entered the army. But it sold only a few dozen copies.

Edgar was successful in the army. He was stationed at Fort Monroe, Virginia, in February 1829, when he received word that Frances was near death from tuberculosis. He immediately left the academy but arrived in Richmond too late. Frances had been buried the day before. (Two years later, Edgar's older brother, William, also died, likely of tuberculosis.) These tragedies, combined with the early death of his mother, clouded Edgar's outlook and greatly influenced his writing.

In 1830, Edgar enrolled at the United States Military Academy at West Point, New York, to become an officer. However, he became bored at the academy and purposely got himself kicked out. After leaving West Point, he moved in with an aunt and her daughter, Virginia, in Baltimore in 1831.

Edgar and Virginia loved each other. Although many accounts say their relationship was mostly like a brother and sister, they were married in 1836. Edgar was twenty-seven and Virginia just thirteen.

They listed her age as twenty-one on the marriage certificate.

Edgar struggled to support his new wife and his aunt. He worked for a while as a magazine editor and literary critic. But he spent the rest of his life trying to make a living as a writer. However, even his most famous works generated very little money during his lifetime.

In 1833, he won fifty dollars from a Baltimore newspaper for the short story "MS. Found in a Bottle." (MS. is an abbreviation for manuscript.) It is about a man who is lost at sea during a terrible storm and writes down the distressing details of his torment—his manuscript—and throws it overboard. The 1839 story "The Fall of the House of Usher" is about twins Roderick and Madeleine Usher and their ill-fated, creepy, old mansion. In 1841's "The Murders in the Rue Morgue," Edgar sent detective C. Auguste Dupin on a mission to solve a series of grisly killings.

In January 1842, Virginia was singing for Edgar and some friends when she coughed up blood. Edgar's heart sank. He had seen it too many times before. He knew it was tuberculosis.

Virginia was sick for the next several years. She would get better one week, then fall back even worse the next. The prospect of her death nearly drove Edgar mad. "I became insane, with long intervals of horrible sanity," he wrote to a friend.

Edgar's "The Masque of the Red Death" was published in the spring of 1842. In the story, a prince and his nobles try to avoid a deadly plague but are done in by a mysterious guest dressed as the Red Death at a masquerade party.

Some experts believe the Red Death represents tuberculosis. Others disagree. But there is little doubt that Edgar's most famous work—"The Raven," published in 1845—was influenced by the impending death of Virginia. When the narrator asks the raven, will he hold the love of his life again? "Quoth the Raven 'Nevermore.'"

Virginia died in 1847. "Deep in earth my love is lying," Edgar wrote, "and I must weep alone." But he didn't want to stay alone. He spent the last couple of years of his life hoping to remarry. He had always held the women in his life in high esteem and, it seemed to him, he couldn't live without a wife. In fact, one of his last great poems, "Annabel Lee," which was published after his death, is believed to be a tribute to the women whom Edgar had loved in his life but who all had died too soon.

Edgar died a strange death in 1849. On September 27, he boarded a steamboat in Richmond to head to New York, with a stop in Baltimore along the way. But six days later, he was found barely conscious on the street outside a tavern in Baltimore. He was talking gibberish and wearing someone else's clothes. He was taken to a hospital, where he died on October 7. He was only forty years old.

Many people have made guesses over the years as to his cause of death. Was he drunk? Had he been drugged? Did he have an unusual disease? No one knows for sure. It remains Edgar's last great mystery.

BRAM STOKER

BRAM STOKER

Six-year-old Bram Stoker wasn't in bed because he was sleepy but because he was sick. He didn't pull the covers up to his eyes because he was cold but because he was scared! He listened as his mother told him spooky stories about screaming banshees, mysterious shape-shifters, and people who had been buried alive.

Some of his mother's stories were terrifying because they were true, like the cholera epidemic of her childhood in Ireland that killed dozens of people every day. Some of her stories were silly, like the mischievous pixies of old Irish folktales. And some were downright creepy, like the legend of the sheriff of Galway—a real-life ancestor of Bram's—who supposedly hanged his own son. But they all fueled an imagination that later helped Bram write a dozen novels and several short-story collections. Most notable was *Dracula*, one of the most famous Gothic horror books of all time and the novel that most shaped the vampire legend we know today.

Bram Stoker was born in 1847 in Clontarf, Ireland. That's a small village in Dublin, the capital city of the country. His given first name was Abraham, but he was always called Bram as a youngster. Bram was the third of seven children born to Abraham and Charlotte Stoker. Bram's father was a civil servant—a government employee—who worked at offices in Dublin Castle. The castle serves as the major government-building complex in Ireland. Charlotte took care of Bram, his four brothers, and two sisters.

Bram was sick for much of his childhood. In fact, he couldn't walk on his own, and he wasn't allowed out of bed for most of his first six years. Doctors weren't really sure what was the matter.

They thought fresh air might do him some good, so sometimes Abraham and Charlotte took him to the countryside. Sometimes, they took him to church on Sundays. The rest of the time, Bram spent at home.

When Bram wasn't listening to his mother's stories, he read as many books as he could. And he let his imagination run wild. "I was naturally thoughtful," he would say after becoming a writer. His long illness "gave opportunity for many thoughts, which were fruitful in later years." This was Bram's way of saying that he spent plenty of time alone with his thoughts, which may have helped him develop stories later in life.

And then suddenly, when he was seven, Bram was no longer ill. No one knew exactly why. Doctors thought it was a miracle. Bram didn't care about the reason. He just knew that now he could go to school, play outside, and be with other kids.

Bram turned out to be an excellent student. That wasn't surprising because he read so much during the years when he was confined to his bed. But he also turned out to be a great athlete. Bram grew to be tall, strong, and broad shouldered.

When he was sixteen, Bram went to Trinity College in Dublin. He graduated in 1870 with a degree in mathematics. He also was a star runner, rugby player, rower, and gymnast. After Trinity College, Bram followed in his father's footsteps by becoming a civil servant at Dublin Castle. Bram eventually became the inspector of petty sessions there. That meant he was in charge of making sure that hundreds of small-case legal courts all over Ireland ran smoothly.

Bram was apparently pretty good at a difficult job, but he was bored. He preferred the excitement of going to the theater. He also liked to write. So he figured out a way to combine the two things he enjoyed so much: He began writing theater reviews for the *Dublin Evening Mail* newspaper. That set in motion a series of events that led to his writing the novel *Dracula*.

In the early 1870s, Bram wrote a review of a local performance of Shakespeare's *Hamlet*. The star of that play was Henry Irving, one of England's most famous actors. Irving was a big star with a big personality— and a big ego. Bram's review praised him. When Irving read it, he was flattered. He asked to meet with the author the next time he was in Dublin.

Bram and Irving met in 1876. Soon afterward, the actor invited Bram to a dinner party with several other people. At the party, Irving stood and read "The Dream of Eugene Aram," a ballad by British poet Thomas Hood.

Bram was spellbound by the reading. And when Irving was done, Bram was so excited that he "burst out into something like a violent fit of hysterics." That only fed Irving's considerable ego, and the two became good friends.

In 1878, Irving asked Bram to work for him as a personal assistant and business manager at the Lyceum Theatre in London, England, which the actor was in charge of. Bram accepted the job, and he and his wife, Florence, moved to London that year. He became Irving's right-hand man, answering dozens of letters every day, arranging for travel and accommodations, greeting customers at the theater, and overseeing a staff of nearly fifty. Somehow, Bram still found time to write on the side. His early efforts included a collection of stories for children called *Under the Sunset*, published in 1881. The stories are fairy tales about faraway lands. They are notable for their contribution to the history of fantasy literature but offer little indication of the scarier side of Bram's writing, still to come.

Meanwhile, Bram's theater job enabled him to meet interesting people from all over the world. They included US presidents William McKinley and Theodore Roosevelt, writers Oscar Wilde and Sir Arthur Conan Doyle, and poet Walt Whitman. At one dinner at the Lyceum sometime in the 1880s, Bram was introduced to Ármin Vámbéry, a native of the Kingdom of Hungary and an expert in Eastern European history and culture. Vámbéry told Bram folktales of the region, including the myth of the vampire. The vampire was a strange "undead" being who sailed to a distant land in search of new victims to spread his curse. Other elements from Vámbéry— such as vampires needing to sleep in a coffin filled with dirt from their homeland, their aversion to garlic, and death by wooden stake—eventually made their way into the story Bram was writing.

Bram worked on *Dracula* for seven years, beginning in 1890. The book was published to great reviews, although it was not a huge best seller at the time. Certainly, it didn't make Bram rich. He wrote several more novels over the next fourteen years, including *The Lady of the Shroud*, which was published in 1909, and *The Lair of the White Worm* in 1911. However, it was not until after Bram's death at age sixty-four in 1912 that *Dracula* became known around the world through many movie and theater adaptations.

Over the years, scholars have argued over who was Bram's inspiration for Dracula. For a long time, it was believed to be Vlad the Impaler, a fifteenth-century Romanian ruler who was actually nicknamed Dracula. Vlad the Impaler was a brutal tyrant who tortured his enemies. However, Bram likely only took Vlad the Impaler's nickname for his story.

Bram's description of Dracula comes from the details the character Jonathan Harker provides for the reader in the novel. Harker met with a tall, old man dressed in black from head to toe. He had a high nose and "peculiarly arched nostrils; with lofty domed forehead, and hair growing scantily round the temples, but profusely elsewhere."

That physical description of Dracula sounds a lot

like Bram's boss, Henry Irving! However, the story of Dracula likely sprang from his imagination inspired by his own mother's horrific tales of the undead, heard in his childhood. Those stories, combined with a life in the theater and a fascination with the folktales and superstitions of Eastern Europe, led Bram Stoker to write one of the most enduring horror novels of all time.

H. P. LOVECRAFT

H. P. LOVECRAFT

There is a line in H. P. Lovecraft's short story "The Call of Cthulhu" (usually said, "cuh-THOO-loo") in which the narrator describes a small statue of the frightful sea creature as a monster that "only a diseased fancy could conceive." In other words, a monster so frightful that only someone with a twisted imagination could create it—which pretty much sums up the author of the story!

Cthulhu is a sort of combination dragon and octopus that emerges from the sea. It is "miles high," with a scaly body and long wings. If that all sounds a little weird, it is appropriate that "The Call of Cthulhu" first appeared in *Weird Tales* magazine in 1928. The story went on to spawn an entire fictional universe called the Cthulhu Mythos. Many writers have contributed to the Cthulhu Mythos over the decades, but it first sprang from the imagination of H. P. Lovecraft.

Although he produced hundreds of poems, dozens of short stories, and several novellas (short books), H. P. was hardly known at all during his lifetime. Not many of his stories and books were printed while he was alive. Those that were, sold very few copies.

H. P. Lovecraft was born Howard Phillips Lovecraft in Providence, Rhode Island, in 1890. His father, Winfield, was a traveling salesman. His mother was named Susie. H. P. was only three when his father became mentally ill and was sent to an asylum. H. P. never saw him again.

Susie and H. P. moved in with her father, a successful businessman named Whipple Van Buren Phillips. They lived in a big house in Providence. H. P. was often sick and didn't go to school much. But his grandfather had a huge library. H. P. read everything he could, including the stories of horror writer Edgar Allan Poe. He took an interest in science, especially anatomy (the study of the internal workings and bodily structure of living things). At night, his grandfather would tell him ghost stories. They gave him nightmares—but also ideas for his own stories.

However, when H. P.'s grandfather died in 1904, his world changed dramatically. Susie couldn't afford to stay in the big house. She and H. P. went to live with two of his aunts in a much smaller house.

During his teenage years, H. P. rarely talked to anyone but his family. He didn't go out at all during the daytime. He was distrustful and thought terrible things about Jewish people and other minority groups. He was socially awkward. Instead of talking with people, he wrote letters nonstop. Some reports say he wrote up to one hundred thousand letters in his lifetime—perhaps up to ten letters per day! And some of those letters were dozens of pages long. H. P. wrote so many letters to the editor of one magazine that he caught the attention of the United Amateur Press Association (UAPA). The UAPA hired him in 1914 to write stories. Being part of the UAPA helped him make some writer friends.

H. P. also began writing poems and short stories to sell on his own. In 1917, when he was twenty-seven, he wrote a short story called "Dagon." It was published in 1919. Dagon is about a sailor who is prepared to kill himself. "I am writing this under an appreciable mental strain, since by tonight I shall be no more," the story begins. "Penniless, and at the end of my supply of the drug which alone makes life endurable, I can bear the torture no longer; and shall cast myself from this garret window into the squalid street below."

The sailor is upset because of a terrifying sea creature he encountered. It was as frightening as the kind of sea monster that H. P. would later write about in "The Call of Cthulhu."

Shortly after H. P.'s mother died in 1921, he met a woman named Sonia Greene at a writers' convention. They married in 1924 and moved to New York, although the marriage did not last long. By 1926, H. P. returned to Providence.

Back in Rhode Island, H. P. did some of the best writing of his life. It included short stories such as

"The Dunwich Horror" and "The Haunter of the Dark" for *Weird Tales*, plus novellas like *At the Mountains of Madness* and *The Shadow Out of Time*. Still, he made little money from any of it. One of his last books, *The Shadow Over Innsmouth*, sold only a couple of hundred copies. Late in his life, H. P. didn't even have enough money for food. Instead, he often spent what little he had to cover the postage for his letters.

In one of those many thousands of letters, he explained to a fellow writer how to properly say the name of his most famous creation. While "cuh-THOO-loo" has become the most commonly accepted way, H. P. said there was no way to say Cthulhu in human terms. "The name of the hellish entity was invented by beings whose vocal organs were not like man's," he wrote in 1934, "hence it has no relation to the human speech equipment. The syllables were determined by a physiological equipment wholly unlike ours, hence could never be uttered perfectly by human throats."

It was only after H. P.'s death from cancer at the age of forty-six in 1937 that his writing became famous. Fellow writer August Derleth started a publishing house in the late 1930s just to give H. P.'s books and stories new life. They first became widely popular in Europe after World War II, then in the United States after 1950.

And H. P.'s writing lives on today. "The Call of Cthulhu" alone inspired board games, video games, books, movies, and television shows in the worlds of horror, fantasy, and science fiction. Writers such as Stephen King and Neil Gaiman grew up reading H. P.'s stories and books. They have credited him for influencing their work.

"Dagon" and "The Call of Cthulhu" both featured enormous sea creatures. However, H. P. didn't limit his monsters to the sea. Elder Things are strange alien beings who can change form and become invisible. Shoggoths are shape-shifting forms of a thick, jellylike substance. Old Ones are barrel-shaped, six-foot-tall beings with a five-pointed head and an eye at each point.

According to H. P.'s stories, what his creatures have in common is that they are beyond the ability of humans to understand. And if we could come close to understanding them, the horror of it would drive us mad.

However, H. P. is less known for particular monsters or for any individual works than he is for the world they conjure. It is a world in which human beings are not the enemy of such creatures but rather a lower life form. This feeling even has a name: Lovecraftian horror. In Lovecraftian horror, humans just don't matter in the larger scope of the universe.

That is perhaps the greatest reason why H. P.'s work is so frightening.

DAPHNE DU MAURIER

DAPHNE DU MAURIER

Most of the time, Daphne du Maurier was a strong and self-assured woman. But one day in the 1930s, she discovered some old love letters between her husband and a former girlfriend. There should not have been any reason for these letters to disturb Daphne. They were from the days before she and Frederick Browning were married. And their marriage was a loving one that eventually produced three children, two girls and a boy. Nevertheless, the letters bothered Daphne. Did her husband still think about his old girlfriend? Why would he have kept them?

Daphne, upset over her discovery, then did what any good writer would do—she turned it into a best-selling novel! The novel, *Rebecca*, turned out to be the signature book of Daphne's distinguished literary career. Over more than half a century of writing, she produced seventeen novels and dozens of short stories, plus several plays and nonfiction books.

Daphne du Maurier was born in 1907 in the Regent's Park area of London, England—an upscale neighborhood where many famous people have lived. The du Maurier family was a very creative one. Daphne's parents, Gerald and Muriel, were actors. Gerald was the first Captain Hook in a stage play of *Peter Pan* in the early 1900s. Daphne had an older sister, Angela, and a younger sister, Jeanne. Angela grew up to be an artist and Jeanne, a painter.

Daphne's imagination was sparked by books at a young age. She could read by the time she was four years old, and in her childhood, she read classics like *Treasure Island, Robinson Crusoe, The Strange Case of Dr. Jekyll and Mr. Hyde, Jane Eyre* and many more.

She also noticed the joy that her father, to whom she was very close, took from acting. "I saw why [he] liked to dress up and pretend to be someone else," she said. "I began to do it myself." She and her sisters acted out the books they read or performed their own plays. Sometimes their audience included leading actors and actresses of the time or writers like J. M. Barrie, who created Peter Pan.

In her teen years, Daphne was educated in France. She went on sailing trips with her friends and vacationed all over Europe. She had no worries about money. It all added up to "a world of make-believe," she said. She could have remained in that world, living off her family's fortune and traveling around the globe. Instead, she used the imagination cultivated by reading and playacting to create her own make-believe world through writing. The result was some of the most revered work in British literature, including a couple of horror classics.

Daphne's earliest short stories were rejected by a local publishing house, but in 1931 her first novel was published. *The Loving Spirit* was about four generations involved in the shipping business in the Cornwall area of England. The book was well received by critics, but for Daphne, its most important reader turned out to be Sir Frederick Browning. A war hero who came to be known as the "father of the British airborne forces," Browning did something that sounds like it was straight out of a novel: After reading the book's descriptions of Cornwall, he decided he had to see it for himself. Though stationed in the army in the village of Pirbright, about two hundred miles to the northeast, in 1931 he made his way to the coast and set out in his own boat for Cornwall. He returned in April 1932 and decided he had to meet the author of *The Loving Spirit*. They met, fell in love, and were married just three months later.

Daphne wrote three more novels over the next several years, including *Jamaica Inn*, a 1936 murder mystery that was made into a movie three years later. But it was *Rebecca* that made her the most famous female author at that time in England.

Inspired by those love letters Daphne once found, *Rebecca* tells of a young woman who meets a rich man whose wife died in an apparent boating accident one year earlier. They marry and move into the man's large house. The house is called Manderley, and it is run by a strict, and at times creepy, housekeeper named Mrs. Danvers. The story is about suspected murder, and it reveals the jealousy a young wife has over the memory of her husband's first wife (named Rebecca) and the jealousy that Mrs. Danvers has over a new wife moving into Manderley.

Rebecca was an instant sensation upon publication in August 1938. The initial print run of twenty thousand copies sold out immediately. By the end of the first month, it had sold forty thousand copies. The book has never been out of print, with sales totals reaching into the millions. The book was made into a movie in 1940 and won the Academy Award for Best Picture.

The horror of Daphne's most well-known story isn't of the blood-and-gore kind. Although a thriller complete with a huge mansion and a sinister housekeeper, there are no actual ghosts in *Rebecca*. There is just the memory of a dead woman whose presence lives on, and the atmosphere of terror that it brings to the new bride.

Creating such dreadful, eerie feelings was Daphne's first goal when writing a book or a story. But she could write more obvious horror, too.

This is most evident in short stories she wrote later in her career.

In "The Birds," a British farmer is standing on the beach, looking out over the water at what he thinks are choppy waves. "Then he saw them," Daphne wrote. "The gulls. Out there, riding the seas. What he had thought at first to be the white caps of the waves were gulls. Hundreds, thousands, tens of thousands." It is a terrifying image. Huge flocks of previously harmless birds have turned aggressive and are creating havoc all over England. The scene was brought to life dramatically in a 1963 movie of the same name based on Daphne's story. In the end, the farmer is unable to keep the violent birds from destroying his home and family.

Daphne's 1971 short story "Don't Look Now" was also made into a movie. In that story, a married British couple travels to Italy for work after their young daughter dies from an illness. Two mysterious old women tell the couple they see their deceased daughter sitting with them at the dinner table. The husband of the couple, John, begins having his own visions and eventually is murdered in a terrible fashion—

a knife hurled across the room into his throat. "What a bloody silly way to die," he thinks as the realization of his doom sets in.

It's a gruesome but thrilling story that is a triumph of Daphne's vivid imagination, which only grew more vibrant and active up to her death at age eighty-one in 1989. She may have grown up in a formal British household, but her imagination was wild and free!

SHIRLEY JACKSON

SHIRLEY JACKSON

In 1948, Alfred Knopf broke his leg while skiing in Vermont. Knopf, a major New York publisher, had taken a pretty serious fall. "Get well" letters poured in from writers, colleagues, and friends around the country.

It is unlikely that any of those letters came from writer Shirley Jackson. In fact, Shirley always said she had caused the accident from her home, many miles away in North Bennington, Vermont! Knopf was in a contract dispute at the time with Shirley's husband, the writer Stanley Edgar Hyman. And Shirley was angry.

So she made a voodoo doll of Alfred Knopf, and she stuck pins in it. Knopf suffered his fall, and Shirley gleefully took the credit.

Of course, Shirley was kidding. But most skiing accidents happen while barreling fast down a slope. Knopf had been going slowly *up* a slope while riding a towrope. And did we mention that Shirley was a witch? She was, according to the jacket cover of one of her books, "Perhaps the only contemporary writer who is a practicing amateur witch." She had to wait until Knopf traveled into Vermont from New York, she claimed, because she was not allowed to practice witchcraft across state lines. More than one reviewer joked that Shirley "writes not with a pen but a broomstick."

Shirley wasn't really a witch, and she didn't really write with a broomstick, but she did little to dispel such notions, either. It was a helpful image for her to cultivate as she penned horror novels such as *The Haunting of Hill House* and *We Have Always Lived in the Castle*. However, her most famous work was the short story "The Lottery." It is a psychologically terrifying thriller set in more modern times. "The Lottery" is one of the most widely read short stories ever. Most American students have studied "The Lottery" at one time or another since it was first published in the *New Yorker* magazine in 1948.

Shirley Jackson was born in San Francisco, California, in 1916. She grew up in nearby Burlingame, a small suburb just south of the city that was, and remains, home to many upper-middle-class households, like the Jackson's. Shirley's father, Leslie, was an executive at a printing company. Her mother, Geraldine, came from a family of successful architects. They wanted their only daughter (Shirley had a younger brother, Barry) to concentrate on learning to be a proper young lady. However, Shirley was more interested in reading and in writing in her journals than going to parties and dances.

Before Shirley could begin her senior year in high school, her father was transferred to a job on the East Coast. The family moved to Rochester, New York. Shirley eventually went to the University of Rochester and then to Syracuse University.

While at Syracuse, Shirley worked for the school's literary magazine. She not only met her future husband there, but she also published her first short story. "Janice" was about a college student who talks about her attempt at suicide. That story revealed the sort of psychological terror that would turn up in much of Shirley's work over the next quarter of a century, including many of her short stories and her two best-known novels.

If you haven't read "The Lottery," for instance, well . . . we won't give away the plot. But the dread that overcomes the lottery "winner" is unforgettable. What really makes the story so horrifying is that it seems so very real. It takes place in a small town, perhaps just like the Vermont one where Shirley lived. The people seem like normal neighbors who make polite conversation about TV dinners, the weather, and more. The story has become a classic for its commentary on peer pressure and groupthink, social traditions, and small-town life.

Shirley's *The Haunting of Hill House*, published in 1959, is in many ways a classic haunted-house story. Ghosts roam the halls, unknown forces try to burst through locked doors, and strange writing appears on the walls. But it is the way these mysteries play on the minds of the characters inside the house that is the most terrifying.

The Haunting of Hill House is a favorite of many horror writers who came after Shirley. Ramsey Campbell called it "the greatest of all haunted house novels." Neil Gaiman listed it as the scariest book of fiction he ever read. Joe Hill calls it the ghost story on which all other ghost stories are built.

Shirley never believed in ghosts herself. Instead, her own anxiety haunted her. This shows up in her journal writing, which was not confined to one book. She wrote in different journals in different voices, depending on her mood and personality of the day. She even gave her different moods different names. Late in her short life, she battled agoraphobia, which is the fear of public places and crowds. And she also suffered from nightmares.

Shirley may not have believed in ghosts, but she had hundreds of volumes about witchcraft among the more than twenty-five thousand books in her and her husband's library. She even wrote a book for children about the Salem witch trials of the late seventeenth century.

Shirley had four children of her own. She was a great cook and a loving mother, but she hated housework. She made fun of her own messy style in a pair of fictionalized memoirs called *Life Among the Savages* and *Raising Demons*.

Like many moms, Shirley sang to her "little demons" each night before they went to sleep. Unlike most moms, though, many of her nursery songs were dark and scary. One was an old ballad called "The Grattan Murders," about a man who killed an entire family one by one. Shirley included it in *The Haunting of Hill House*. It begins: "The first was young Miss Grattan / She tried not to let him in / He stabbed her with a corn knife / That's how his crimes begin."

Shirley was only forty-eight when she died of a heart attack in 1965. In all, she wrote six novels and published seven short-story collections. However, she'll always be remembered mostly for "The Lottery."

Perhaps the only thing more horrifying than "The Lottery" is the number of letters Shirley received from people who thought the story was true, or at least based on true events. "People at first were not so much concerned with what the story meant,"

Shirley wrote in *Come Along with Me*, a collection of her writing that was published three years after her death. "What they wanted to know was where these lotteries were held, and whether they could go there and watch."

And that may have been the scariest thing Shirley Jackson ever wrote.

ROBERT BLOCH

ROBERT BLOCH

Robert was a teenager in the early 1930s when he wrote a letter to H. P. Lovecraft. Robert never missed an issue of *Weird Tales*, and Lovecraft was a major contributor to the magazine. Robert wanted to know how he could obtain copies of past issues of the magazine featuring Lovecraft's stories. And so began a regular correspondence between the two.

By the fourth letter or so, Lovecraft complimented Robert on his writing style. "Would you like to write some stories?" Lovecraft wrote. "I'd be glad to comment on them."

How could Robert refuse?! He sent a couple of short stories in and received encouragement from Lovecraft. Robert bought a used typewriter when he graduated from high school. "I sat down and I began to work," he said. "Six weeks later I sold my first story to *Weird Tales*."

His story, called "The Feast in the Abbey," was printed in the January 1935 issue of *Weird Tales*. At just seventeen, Robert was a professional writer! As a way of thanking Lovecraft for helping him, Robert asked permission to use him as a character in the 1935 short story "The Shambler from the Stars"—a character that is killed. By all means! Lovecraft responded. Robert could feel free to "portray, murder, annihilate, disintegrate, transfigure, metamorphose, or otherwise manhandle" his character in the story. A couple of months later, Lovecraft wrote a story called "The Haunter of the Dark," in which an alien kills a character based on Robert.

Robert's career took off. Over the next six decades, he turned out a seemingly endless stream of horror, fantasy, and weird fiction. He wrote more than twenty-five novels and four hundred short stories. He wrote for radio, for popular television shows such as *Alfred Hitchcock Presents* and *Star Trek*, and for more than a dozen horror films. And he always will be remembered for his 1959 novel *Psycho*, which led to a blockbuster movie of the same name the following year.

Robert Bloch was born in Chicago in 1917 to Ray and Stella Bloch. His sister, Winifred, was born in 1919. The family moved to nearby Maywood, Illinois, when Robert was five, and several years later to Milwaukee, Wisconsin.

Robert was nine when he went to the movies alone at night for the first time. He saw the horror classic *The Phantom of the Opera*, about a mysterious, disfigured man who lives beneath the Paris Opera House. "When I ran all the way home through the dark after the film had ended, the image that floated behind me was the Phantom's face. He kept me company in bed and haunted my dreams." Robert was hooked. After that, he went to see as many horror movies as he could, like *The Bat* and *The Cat and the Canary*.

In 1927, Robert was with his family at a train

station in Chicago when his aunt Lil, his father's sister, offered to buy him any magazine he wanted. He chose *Weird Tales*, which featured an evil-looking man on the cover and stories like "Creeping Shadows" and "The Man with a Thousand Legs" inside. He read every word.

Robert graduated from Lincoln High School in Milwaukee in 1934 and began his writing career. In addition to his short stories, he worked as a copywriter for an advertising firm and on politician Carl Zeidler's successful 1939 campaign for mayor of Milwaukee. He adapted many of his stories into fifteen-minute radio shows in the 1940s, and his first novel, a thriller called *The Scarf*, was published in 1947.

In 1958, Robert wrote a short story called "That Hell-Bound Train" for *The Magazine of Fantasy & Science Fiction*. It is a deal-with-the-devil story in which a man is granted one wish by a train conductor. In exchange, he must ride the train, which is bound for hell, when he dies. The man's wish is to stop time. However, he can never decide at what moment to use his power, and he eventually dies. He boards the train and decides to use it then, so the train never reaches hell.

In September 1959, "That Hell-Bound Train" won the Hugo Award for Best Short Story. The Hugo Awards are presented each year to the best works in science fiction and fantasy. Earlier that same year, what became Robert's best-known book, *Psycho*, was published.

Psycho is a terrifying story of a middle-aged man, Norman Bates, who runs a struggling old hotel with his mother—or does he? When a woman comes to stay at the hotel for the night, Bates, dressed as his mother, breaks in while she is showering. In a scene chillingly depicted in the 1960 movie, he brandishes a large knife menacingly and then kills her. Bates eventually is caught. Because he is psychotic—he has trouble distinguishing good from evil—he is sent to a mental institution.

In Robert's book, the shower scene is intense and frightening. On the movie screen, it is gory and bloody. Robert was no longer a fan of horror movies. In his youth, the older black-and-white films created a certain atmosphere to scare audiences. Part of the thrill was what the audience didn't see but could only imagine. Now movies were starting to rely on showing graphic, bloody violence. He would not go see them. "There is a distinction to be made between that which inspires terror and that which inspires nausea," he said.

Robert's writing was undergoing a change, too. Many of his early horror and weird-fiction stories were tales of the supernatural, like the cat possessed by an old witch that rips out a boy's tongue in 1948's "Catnip." But with *Psycho*, he moved into the realm of psychological terror, as he came to believe that "real horror is not in the shadows, but in that twisted little world inside our own skulls." He stayed with that theme in another best-selling book, *American Gothic*, which was published in 1974. *American Gothic* was not a true story but was based on a real-life serial killer.

Robert's world was not so twisted that he lost his sense of humor. "Despite my ghoulish reputation," he once said, "I really have the heart of a small boy. I keep it in a jar on my desk."

Robert died of cancer at age seventy-seven in 1994. He won dozens of awards in his long career, including the 1989 Bram Stoker Award for Lifetime Achievement in horror writing. Still, he never forgot the kindness that H. P. Lovecraft showed him in his teen years. Although the two never met, they were friends and pen pals until Lovecraft's death at just forty-six in 1937. "Would you say that you owe your career to him?" an interviewer asked Robert after he had been writing for nearly half a century.

"I most certainly do!" Robert said. "And I've never ceased to be grateful to him for it."

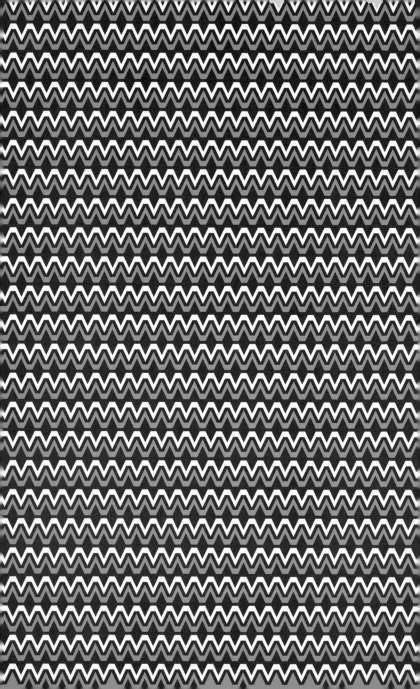

THOMAS HARRIS

THOMAS HARRIS

Thomas Harris's Hannibal Lecter is one of the creepiest villains in horror writing. "I ate his liver with some fava beans" and a glass of red wine, he tells an FBI investigator in a memorable encounter in Thomas's 1988 book, *The Silence of the Lambs*.

Hannibal has joined Frankenstein's monster, Dracula, Pennywise, and Cthulhu as one of the most iconic monsters and villains ever put on paper. But Dr. Frankenstein's creation is built of body parts and chemistry, and Dracula is one of the undead. Pennywise is a supernatural shape-shifter, and

Cthulhu is a mythic creature from the bottom of the sea. Hannibal is different because he is human—a respected psychiatrist who is also a serial killer. He is perhaps the biggest monster of them all.

Unlike those other hideous characters, very little is known about Hannibal's creator. The author of six books that in total have sold more than fifty million copies, Thomas is a quiet man who prefers to stay out of the spotlight.

Some authors are very public figures, and some are not. Although by all accounts a polite, good-humored Southern gentleman who loves to cook and has a soft spot for animals, Thomas Harris doesn't go on book tours or talk about himself very often. In 2019, he surprised readers by granting an interview to the *New York Times*. It was his first major interview in forty-three years!

Thomas was born as William Thomas Harris III in Jackson, Tennessee, in 1940. His father, William, was an electrical engineer. His mother, Polly, was a teacher. When his father went off to serve in the military during World War II, Polly and Thomas moved to Rich, Mississippi. Thomas was quiet and shy as a child and not popular with other kids. So he turned to books. He not only read them, but he also found another clever use for books. He stacked them up and built a fort—a private space of his own.

After graduating from high school in Mississippi, Thomas went on to earn a degree in English from Baylor University in Waco, Texas. He wrote for the newspaper the *Waco Herald-Tribune* before moving to New York City in 1968 to work for the Associated Press (AP). At the AP, he covered all sorts of crimes ranging from robberies to murders.

It was also at the AP that he and two other writers came up with a book idea: It was a suspense novel about a terrorist attack at the Super Bowl. Although all three men shared the idea, Thomas eventually wrote the book, called *Black Sunday*, which was published in 1975. When it was made into a movie two years later, Thomas had earned enough money to begin writing books full-time.

His next effort, called *Red Dragon*, was published in 1981. It tells the story of a search for a serial killer nicknamed "the Tooth Fairy" who is murdering entire families. Hannibal first appears in *Red Dragon* as a prison inmate who advises the FBI in the hunt for the Tooth Fairy. Hannibal is introduced as a criminally insane serial killer who ate the flesh of his victims. "Hannibal the Cannibal" turned out to be so intriguing and popular a character that Thomas made him the focus of his next several books.

By far the most famous of those books was *The Silence of the Lambs*. In this story, another serial killer is on the loose. He is nicknamed "Buffalo Bill," and he kills young women. While he isn't a cannibal, he is very interested in collecting the skin of his victims. It's pretty gruesome stuff.

When the FBI tries to catch Buffalo Bill before he can claim another victim, it again turns to Hannibal to better learn how the criminal mind works. A former psychiatrist, Hannibal can be charming and sophisticated when he wants to be. He is incredibly smart and has sophisticated tastes in music and food. But he is also a sociopath: selfish, antisocial, and incapable of considering the feelings of others.

The FBI needs Hannibal's help, but he's not going to make it easy for them. When he lies about knowing that the serial killer's name is "Louis Friend," he has rearranged the letters in "iron sulfide." That is also known as fool's gold. Hannibal is sending investigators on a wild-goose chase.

Thomas wrote some gory scenes in the book. While writing, he called his mother every night. (His father had died while Thomas was writing *Red Dragon.*) He told her so many grisly details of the scenes he had written that day that it kept her awake at night.

It was eleven years before Thomas's character returned in the novel *Hannibal* in 1999. *Hannibal Rising* followed in 2006. Then came *Cari Mora* in 2019—Thomas's first book without the character of Hannibal in it since *Black Sunday*. *Cari Mora* is a crime thriller about a young woman who has to outwit another insane killer on the hunt for hidden gold.

Each of the Hannibal books, as well as *Red Dragon* and *Black Sunday*, were made into movies. (*Red Dragon* was called *Manhunter* at the movies.) The most successful was *The Silence of the Lambs*. It was a box-office smash. Audiences loved it, and critics did, too. *The Silence of the Lambs* is one of the few movies in history to sweep all of the top five Academy Awards, which are presented annually for excellence in the movies. It won the awards for Best Picture, Best Director, Best Actor, Best Actress, and Best Adapted Screenplay. In 2003, the American Film Institute ranked Hannibal number one on its list of the top villains in movie history.

How did someone whom his mother once called "the most gentle person I have ever known" make up such a ghastly character? That is the question Thomas heard from reporters early in his writing career. One even suggested it must take a mentally unstable person to make up such a convincing one. Perhaps that's the reason Thomas stopped giving interviews for so long. Instead, he says, he wants his writing to do the talking.

So we'll let Hannibal answer the question for Thomas. "Nothing happened to me, Officer Starling," Hannibal tells the FBI investigator who is visiting him in jail in *The Silence of the Lambs*. "I happened. You can't reduce me to a set of influences."

ANNE RICE

ANNE RICE

Anne Rice was carefully placed in her coffin. The coffin was loaded onto the back of a horse-drawn funeral carriage at Lafayette Cemetery No. 1 in New Orleans. The carriage pulled away from the cemetery, rattling along a bumpy road. After a short ride, the carriage pulled up alongside . . . a bookstore?

The famous author wasn't dead. This was the summer of 1995, and fifty-three-year-old Anne decided it was about time she had her own jazz funeral. That is a New Orleans tradition in which the life of a person who has died is celebrated with music and dancing. A jazz band leads a procession to and from a funeral home. Family and friends of the dead person follow. Then the carriage or car carrying the coffin comes next. The music starts out slow and sad. Soon it becomes lively and happy. The people twirl and dance, waving handkerchiefs or fancy umbrellas.

Anne wanted to know what it was like to have a jazz funeral without the inconvenient part of actually being dead. And she had a book signing to attend for her new novel, called *Memnoch the Devil*. What better way for an author who writes about the supernatural to arrive at her book signing than in a coffin?

Anne Rice is from New Orleans, where jazz funerals began as a way to honor musicians who have died. She was born there in 1941. Her given name was Howard O'Brien. She was named after her father, Howard, who worked for the postal service. Her mother was Kay. Anne hated her name. It was a boy's name. So one day in the first grade, she asked her teacher to start calling her Anne. That was a name she liked. Anne's last name came from the man she married in 1961, Stan Rice.

Anne had a sister, Alice, who was two years

older than Anne. The family lived with Kay's mom in an area of New Orleans called the Irish Channel. As a youngster, Anne liked to take long walks around the city. She admired the big oak trees, the stately mansions with their elegant columns, and the mysterious air created by Gothic architecture all around. "The place is positively spooky," Anne says.

One of the spookiest things about New Orleans is its cemeteries. They are unique because the dead are buried in aboveground tombs. Most of the city is at or below sea level, which made it too difficult for underground burials. Anne remembers walking through the maze-like cemetery grounds with her parents and her sister, her father pointing out families that died from frightening illnesses such as yellow fever.

Anne found plenty of inspiration for her spine-tingling stories while walking through those cemeteries and streets of New Orleans. But she also learned about writing from reading the classic works of authors such as Charles Dickens, William Shakespeare, and the Brontë sisters. As a child, Anne also tried to read Bram Stoker's *Dracula* but found it too scary. She returned the book to the library after only a few chapters! Later, she read modern horror writers, like Stephen King.

Kay O'Brien died when Anne was a teenager, and the family moved to Texas, where Anne met and married Stan Rice. In 1962, she and her husband moved to California, where she earned a degree in political science from San Francisco State University.

In the early 1970s, the couple's five-year-old daughter, Michele, died of leukemia. "It was a nightmare," Anne says. She threw herself into her writing. The result was one of the best-selling horror books ever written, *Interview with the Vampire*.

Before her daughter's death, Anne wrote a short story about a vampire. She wanted to explore what a vampire must think about sucking blood and taking a human life to keep itself alive. She wrote it from the viewpoint of a two-hundred-year-old vampire telling his life story to a reporter.

After Michele's death, Anne revisited the story. She expanded it and turned it into a novel. One of the characters was a five-year-old girl who is turned into a vampire. "I didn't know it at the time but it was all about my daughter," Anne said many years later, "the loss of her and the need to go on living when faith is shattered."

At first, several publishers turned down *Interview with the Vampire*. Anne eventually sold it to Knopf, and the book was available in stores in the spring of 1976. Book critics didn't love *Interview with the Vampire*, but readers sure did. The book earned nearly $1 million in paperback sales alone. A dozen sequels followed, from *The Vampire Lestat* in 1985 to *Blood Communion: A Tale of Prince Lestat* in 2018.

Anne also wrote historical fiction and other horror series featuring witches and wolves. But she is best known for her series of vampire books, which have helped her sell an estimated one hundred million books around the world.

Many of Anne's stories are set in New Orleans, where she returned to live from 1988 until 2004, less than two years after her husband died. She was inspired by what she calls the "haunted ambience" of the city. She also had other creepy—and more personal—things to fuel her imagination, like the coffin in which she rode to her book signing (it was her coffin), her collection of more than one thousand dolls (she arranged them around the house to appear in conversation with one another) and the mansion where she lived (which once had been an orphan asylum).

She also admits that she is obsessed with sin, death, and fallen angels—subjects that are explored throughout her writing. In the Old Testament tradition in the Bible, fallen angels were cast out of heaven for rebelling against God.

The vampires in Anne's writing are fallen angels. "I can't write about a villain for too long without trying to find the good side of that villain," she once told an interviewer, "the side that will confuse us as we try to judge them." She created a new kind of vampire, one who searches for a reason for their existence and debates the nature of good and evil. Indeed, Anne says, they might have been good "if they hadn't been seduced by a concept that sounds irresistible, but is really a nightmare."

The not-so-subtle idea is that such a thing could happen to any of us despite our good intentions. Is that the ultimate horror in Anne's writing?

R. L. STINE

R. L. STINE

Bob Stine, better known to readers around the world as R. L. Stine, laughed as he watched his young son, Matt, struggle with his Halloween costume. Matt had tried on a Frankenstein mask, and now it was stuck! Matt tugged and tugged, and Bob laughed and laughed—and started taking notes. "I should have helped him, right?" Bob says. It might have been terrifying, but it was funny, too. And it was going to make a great story for Goosebumps, he thought.

Bob was right. Not long after, in 1993, *The Haunted Mask* became another addition to the enormously successful Goosebumps series of horror books for children. It is about a young girl who buys a Halloween mask from a store. She discovers that after putting the mask on, she starts acting mean. Then she realizes that she can't take it off. The mask has become part of her.

The Haunted Mask was the eleventh Goosebumps book. Over the next several years, Bob wrote fifty-one more books in the original Goosebumps series, which was selling as many as four million copies a month! And yet, Bob never set out to write horror stories at all. He always figured his future would be in making people laugh, not scream. In the end, he did both.

Bob was born in Columbus, Ohio, in 1943. His full name is Robert Lawrence Stine. That's where "R. L." comes from. But he was always called Bob as a kid. "No one ever called me R. L. in my life," he says. Bob was the oldest of Lewis and Anne Stine's three children. His younger brother is Bill, and his sister is Pam.

The Stine family lived in a town called Bexley, just a few miles from Columbus. "We were very poor," Bob says. "I had to wear my cousin's old clothes to school." That made Bob shy and a bit timid. In fact, young Bob was what children of his time might have called a "fraidy-cat." That may sound improbable for someone who makes his living writing scary stories. But Bob was afraid of the dark. He was afraid to jump into a swimming pool. He was afraid of parking his bike in the family garage at night because he was sure there was a monster lurking in there somewhere.

However, Bob wasn't too scared to explore in the attic with his brother, Bill, one day when he was nine years old. Bob found an old typewriter up there. And that typewriter changed Bob's life.

He started making up stories. While his siblings and the other kids in the neighborhood played outside, Bob stayed inside, typing them out. His mother begged him to go outside and play. Bob refused. The world was a lot less scary inside. In fact, it was funnier, too. Bob was writing funny stories. He had a knack for it. He began typing funny stories for his friends. He added some drawings and stapled the pages together to make a magazine. His friends loved it! His teachers didn't.

It seemed that Bob's future was in writing funny stuff. And for a while, it was. He went to college at

Ohio State University, where he earned a degree in English but spent most of his time writing and editing the school's humor magazine. He moved to New York City after college and wrote funny books and magazines. He even wrote a book called *How to Be Funny*. The book was filled with advice for kids on how to be funny in school and at the dinner table. This was the kind of advice parents weren't too happy with. The book didn't sell well.

One day, a friend who worked in publishing asked Bob to write a horror story for young adults. The result was *Blind Date*, which was printed in 1986. It was the first time Bob used the name R. L. Stine on one of his books.

Blind Date was a big success and led to the entire Fear Street series of books, first published in 1989. The Fear Street books were written for young adults. The stories are about the teenagers in a made-up town called Shadyside. They sometimes include ghosts or witches but are mostly murder mysteries. The Fear Street books include scarier scenes than the Goosebumps books, which Bob would write for younger readers.

At first, Bob wasn't sure how to write horror for younger readers. So he thought back to when he was a shy kid who was fearful of so many things. "Which is bad when you're a kid," he says, "but now it's very helpful. I can remember that feeling of panic and try to convey that in the books."

In the summer of 1992, the first of the Goosebumps books, *Welcome to Dead House*, was published. In *Welcome to Dead House*, a couple of kids and their parents move into a creepy old house. Their entire neighborhood is inhabited by the undead. It might be the scariest of all the Goosebumps books. By the second book in the series, *Stay Out of the Basement*, Bob found ways to add some funny moments to his stories, too.

After that, Bob wrote and published almost one Goosebumps book each month. He always started with his idea for the title. He then outlined a story based on that title. For instance, one day he was walking his dog in the park. He thought about when someone is getting ready to take a picture. But he didn't think, "Say, cheese!" Instead, he thought, "Say cheese and die!" That led him to thinking some more.

"What if there was an evil camera?" he thought. "What if some kids discovered the camera? And what if the camera took pictures of bad things that happened to you a little bit in the future?" The result was book number four in the Goosebumps series, *Say Cheese and Die!*

By that time, Goosebumps was really starting to take off. Kids were back in school, and they started telling one another about this cool new series. Bob's books started selling by the millions and have never stopped. They became so popular, they were made into a television series in the 1990s. In the 2010s, comedian Jack Black starred as Bob in two Goosebumps movies.

In all, Bob has authored more than 330 books—and counting! He still writes almost every day. When it is time to work, he settles into the office in his New York City apartment for inspiration. In one corner, there's a fake, three-foot-long cockroach. ("I tell everyone I caught it under the sink," he says.) In another corner, there's a life-size skeleton standing over the author's desk. (It's wearing a sailor's hat!) Slappy, the famously creepy dummy of the

Goosebumps books, sits in a chair. (An R. L. Stine look-alike dummy sits beside it.)

The office is part horror and part humor. It is the perfect atmosphere for Bob's writing because that combination has made him one of the most popular writers in the world.

STEPHEN KING

STEPHEN KING

Stephen King is often asked a variation of the same question: "What was your childhood like?"

People ask because they want to know "what twisted me to do what I'm doing," he says. "The truth is even more horrible. The answer is nothing. I'm just this way naturally!"

Well, maybe not entirely naturally. There was that time he witnessed the gruesome death of a friend at an early age. There were the comic books and the creepy stories that he read as a youngster. And then there were his fears: spiders, serial killers, sewers, and the number thirteen. (Fear of the number thirteen is actually called triskaidekaphobia).

Stephen took those fears and created stories out of them. His fear of sewers gave rise to the creepy clown Pennywise of the novel *It*. His fear of serial killers spawned *Mr. Mercedes* and others. Huge spider creatures attack people in Stephen's novella *The Mist*.

Such characters and creatures are a huge hit with readers, and Stephen's books are immensely popular. They have sold more than 350 million copies around the world over the past five decades. That makes him the best-selling horror writer of all time—and one of the best-selling writers in any genre ever.

Stephen King was born in Portland, Maine, in 1947. His parents were Donald and Nellie King. Young Stephen was only two when he suffered an emotional trauma: His father went out to buy a pack of cigarettes one day and never returned. Donald didn't want to be part of the family anymore.

After that, Nellie raised Stephen and his older brother, David, herself. They moved around a bit to Illinois, Indiana, and elsewhere, but eventually settled back in Maine.

One day when Stephen was four, he went to play at a friend's house. The house was close to a line of railroad tracks. He soon came back home, pale as a ghost and unwilling to talk the rest of the day. "I would not tell [my mother] why I'd not waited to be picked up or phoned that I wanted to come home," he says. "I would not tell her why my chum's mom hadn't walked me back but had allowed me to come alone." To this day, Stephen does not remember anything that happened. "It turned out that the kid I had been playing with had been run over by a freight train while playing on or crossing the tracks. Years later, my mother told me they had picked up the pieces in a wicker basket."

Steven was not among the popular kids at school. He often felt like an outsider, just like many of the characters in his novels. He spent much of his time reading on his own. He was eleven or twelve when he discovered a box full of old paperbacks his father used to read. He read through all those books, which included the strange horror writing of H. P. Lovecraft. He enjoyed scary stories, especially the ones he found in the comic books "that kids weren't supposed to read," he says. These included *Tales from the Crypt* and *The Vault of Horror*.

Stephen figured he could make up tales just as good as the ones he found in those publications. He began writing stories and submitting them to magazines. One by one, rejection notices came in. For motivation, he kept every one, nailing them to his bedroom wall. He was still a teenager when "the nail in my wall would no longer support the weight of the rejection slips impaled upon it," he wrote. "I replaced the nail with a spike and went on writing."

Stephen was in high school when his first published story, "I Was a Teenage Grave Robber," appeared in *Comics Review* in 1965. He went on to the University of Maine, where he graduated with a degree in English. He also met Tabitha Spruce there. Stephen and Tabitha were married in 1971. They have three children, Naomi, Joe, and Owen. Joe is the successful horror author Joe Hill.

For several years, Stephen and Tabitha struggled to make ends meet. They lived in run-down apartments and drove a beat-up car. They even disconnected their phone to save money. Stephen worked at a gas station, a laundromat, and other jobs before becoming a teacher at Hampden Academy, a high school in Maine. He still wrote whenever he could and sold an occasional short story. He also finished three novels but was unable to sell any of them.

One day in the early 1970s, Stephen had an idea for a story. He wrote one page on his typewriter, then another and another. He read them over—and hated what he read. He balled up the pages and threw them into the trash.

Tabitha noticed the crumpled-up pages in the wastebasket and fished them out. She dusted off the cigarette ashes, smoothed out the paper, and read Stephen's words herself. She thought the story had potential. She encouraged Stephen to expand the story into a book, which became *Carrie*. It was the fourth novel Stephen wrote, but in 1974, it was his first to be published.

Carrie is the story of a teenage girl who can control objects with her mind. She uses that power to get back at the classmates who had been making her life miserable in high school. The hardcover edition was not a big hit. But the next year, Stephen received a telegram from his publisher—he still couldn't afford a telephone—saying that the paperback rights had been sold for $400,000. According to the terms of his contract, half of that went to Stephen.

That large payment from his publisher meant Stephen could now write full-time—and he hasn't stopped writing since. His books are some of modern horror's best-known works, such as 1977's *The Shining*, 1983's *Pet Sematary*, and 1987's *Misery*. All of those books, and many others, were made into movies, too.

Stephen has written more than sixty novels, including seven written under the pen name Richard Bachman. That's an amazing rate of more than one novel per year since *Carrie* hit the shelves. He also has authored hundreds of short stories and several longer stories. He has written screenplays for movies and television. Nearly half of his books have reached number one on the *New York Times* best-seller list. He has won a record thirteen Bram Stoker Awards for achievement in horror writing, including a lifetime achievement award in 2002. He won an Edgar Award in 2015 for best novel for *Mr. Mercedes*.

Sometimes Stephen's own reality has been

almost as scary as his fiction. In the 1980s, he battled drug and alcohol addiction even while churning out novel after novel; he kicked both habits late in the decade. In 1991, a man broke into Stephen's house while Tabitha was home; she escaped and called the police, who found the man hiding in the attic. In 1999, Stephen was hit by a van while out walking near his home; he suffered serious leg and hip injuries that bother him to this day.

Despite all that, and despite a relentless drive to create new characters and produce more content, Stephen easily answers another question he often gets from critics and fans.

"People ask me if I have bad dreams," he once told an interviewer. "The answer is, no, I give them all to somebody else. I sleep well."

CLIVE BARKER

CLIVE BARKER

During his days at summer camp as a young boy in England, Clive Barker couldn't pitch a tent, tie a knot, or play soccer as well as the other kids. But at night around the campfire, he sure could do one thing better than any of them: tell ghost stories. "I knew these imaginative areas where I had authority, where I had some kind of power," he says. "I could tell stories to people, and they would listen."

More than half a century later, he is still telling stories, and people are still listening. Clive is the author of more than a dozen horror or fantasy novels, plus short stories, movies, and plays. He has written for or helped develop comic books and video games based on his work. He says that a much-anticipated new book called *Deep Hill* "is one of the scariest things I've done."

Clive Barker was born in Liverpool in 1952. Clive's father, Leonard, worked for a local business. His mother, Joan, worked for a school. "He was a perfectly normal lad," Joan once told a reporter. Except that when the other kids in school were drawing cute pictures of a mommy and daddy and the sun and the trees, Clive was drawing pictures of a beast devouring other beasts. "These kind of weird things have been going around in my head for as long as I can remember," he says.

Those weird things were nurtured in great part by a selection of reading material that included stories by Edgar Allan Poe. "I remember buying my first edition of *Tales of Mystery and Imagination*," Clive says. *Tales of Mystery and Imagination* is a collection of some of Poe's scariest stories, including "The Pit and the Pendulum," "The Murders in the Rue Morgue" and "The Tell-Tale Heart." Clive was also drawn to his grandmother's stories. She would sit by the fire in her quiet, dark house, with the only other sound the ticking of the clocks, and tell Clive terrible tales about murders, funerals, and burials.

"I don't ever remember a time that I wasn't genuinely interested in horror in some form or another," he says. "It was always the grisly bits of fairy tales that I was interested in. I've always liked fantastical literature of some kind, and I've always liked the darker aspects of that."

Clive decided before he was a teenager that he wanted to pursue a career in the arts, whether it was writing, painting, or making plays or movies. He was encouraged by an English teacher who urged him to feed the creative imagination he displayed in his schoolwork.

After high school, Clive went to the University of Liverpool to study English and philosophy, but he had little interest in his classes. Instead, he focused more on writing and directing plays for a theatrical group he formed. He also began writing a series of short stories that were collected in *Books of Blood*, published in 1984.

Some of the stories in *Books of Blood* are downright grisly. In "The Midnight Meat Train," for instance, one of the compartments on the train is turned into a slaughterhouse where people are killed. The train pulls into a station where strange, humanlike creatures eat the bodies. The entire collection is framed by the short story "The Book of Blood," in which ghosts attack a man and write these scary stories into his flesh.

If that sounds creepy, it is. Famed horror author Stephen King has said about *Books of Blood*: "Some of the stories were so creepily awful that I literally could not read them alone." Early in Clive's career, King also said, "I have seen the future of horror, his name is Clive Barker."

Clive's first novel, *The Hellbound Heart*, was published in 1986. A man in search of ultimate pleasure finds ultimate pain instead. The book introduced demon creatures, called Cenobites, who had "scars that covered every inch of their bodies, flesh cosmetically punctured and sliced," and smelled horrible. One of them had clothes sewn "to and through its skin."

Clive wrote and directed the movie version of *The Hellbound Heart*, called *Hellraiser*, which introduced the leader of the Cenobites as a character who has come to be known as Pinhead. With large pins driven through his head to the skull, Pinhead is Clive's most recognized character.

Like *The Hellbound Heart*, most of Clive's books and stories are very gory and definitely not for younger readers. Clive's lone book for children is 1992's *The Thief of Always*, about a bored ten-year-old who follows a stranger to a kids' paradise—where, of course, things aren't as they seem.

That ten-year-old is a lot like Clive was, with "strange dark imaginings that he never knew quite how to deal with," he says. He has spent the years since finding ways to give shape to those thoughts and images.

Sometimes, that shape has come in the form of novels or stories. Other times, it is in the form of plays, comic books, or paintings. His artwork is sometimes seen on his book covers and occasionally illustrates the text inside.

In 2002, Clive began a series of fantasy books for

young adults with the title *Abarat*. He returned to adult horror with *The Scarlet Gospels* in 2015.

Clive calls the book he is now writing, *Deep Hill*, so scary "because it mingles both imaginative scares (that is to say strange creatures and the like) with very threatening issues about the world we live in."

As grisly as Clive's books and movies are, real life has sometimes been worse. He was only three when he witnessed a skydiver fall to his death at an air show in Liverpool. The man's stunt went wrong, and his emergency parachute didn't open properly. During a 2012 visit to the dentist, poisonous bacteria entered Clive's bloodstream. He fell into a coma (when a person is unconscious but still alive), and doctors thought he might not live. Clive came out of it, but it has been a long, slow recovery ever since.

For sure: Clive's writing has never been boring. Or, to use a word Clive often does, banal. It means lacking in originality or imagination. That is "the thing that scares me," he says. No fears of that, Clive.

NEIL GAIMAN

NEIL GAIMAN

For Neil Gaiman, writing books begins with a simple question: "What if?"

What if . . . the strange door in his house that opened onto a wall actually was a gateway to a whole new world? What if . . . the same family down the road lived in the same house for more than a thousand years? What if . . . the little boy happily playing among the headstones really was at home in the graveyard?

Those kinds of questions are the seeds out of which dozens of books have sprouted and grown.

They have spanned more than three decades and covered a wide variety of styles and formats. Neil mixes a little bit of horror with a little bit of science fiction with a whole lot of fantasy. He writes across a staggering range of media. His work includes novels, graphic novels, comic books, kids books, and television and movie scripts. His credits mostly include fiction, but there is some nonfiction, too.

Neil Gaiman was born in 1960 in an apartment over a grocery store in Portchester, England. Portchester is a small town of about eighteen thousand people located about seventy-five miles southwest of London. Neil's father, David, worked in the store downstairs. It was part of a chain of grocery stores owned by David's father, who had come to England from Belgium around the time World War I started in 1914. Neil's mother, Sheila, was a pharmacist. The family also included Neil's two younger sisters, Claire and Lizzy.

Neil could read by the time he was four. While most of his friends were playing with toy cars or out on the soccer field, Neil was exploring the library or reading a book. One day, he borrowed copies of *The*

Lion, the Witch and the Wardrobe and *The Voyage of the Dawn Treader* from the family next door. Those classics by C. S. Lewis hooked him immediately. For his seventh birthday, he asked his parents for an entire set of Lewis's The Chronicles of Narnia.

There is a sad scene in Neil's 2013 best seller *The Ocean at the End of the Lane* in which the unnamed boy of the story has a party to celebrate his seventh birthday, but no one comes. Streamers are hung and balloons are filled, but the chairs remain empty and the cake, decorated with a book, remains uneaten. The silver lining for the boy is that he gets to spend the entire day lying on his bed reading.

Neil has said that the boy in *The Ocean at the End of the Lane* "is definitely me, age seven. There's nothing that he thinks, there's nothing that he is, there's none of his opinions about books or anything that weren't mine." Of course, the events of the book are made up. They include immortal neighbors, a creepy monster nanny, and birds that eat away at the universe. The birthday scene didn't happen to Neil. But he did spend the entire day that he turned seven on his bed, reading The Chronicles of Narnia. And, just as in the book, the local cake shop really did say that his was the first cake to feature a book on it.

Although Neil was an excellent student, he decided not to go to college. He knew he wanted to write. He began his career as a journalist, writing books and magazine stories about celebrities such as the music group Duran Duran and comedian Terry Jones of Monty Python.

Neil was waiting for a train at London's Victoria Station one day in 1984 when he saw a copy of the comic book *Swamp Thing* that someone had left behind. He had given up comic books because he figured they were "silly schoolboy stuff," but while flipping through the pages of *Swamp Thing*, "all that enthusiasm came back."

He began writing comics and then graphic novels. In 1989, Neil started a comic book series, *The Sandman*, featuring Dream, the ruler of dreams. *The Sandman* ran for seven years. In 1990, Neil teamed with fellow British writer Terry Pratchett on his first novel, *Good Omens*. It is a comedy about an angel and a devil that try to stop the end of the world. Late in the decade, Neil began releasing a string of best sellers: *Stardust* in 1999, followed by *American Gods* and *Coraline*.

The idea for *Coraline* came from a strange door in one of Neil's childhood homes in England. It opened onto a brick wall that separated his house from the house next door. "I used to creep up on it," Neil says, "because I was sure that if I opened the door fast enough, it wouldn't be a brick wall, it would lead somewhere."

Eleven-year-old Coraline finds a similar setup in her own home. "Coraline discovered the door a little while after they moved into the house," the book begins. "The door didn't go anywhere," it is later explained. "It opened onto a brick wall."

But Coraline discovers that if she opens the door when she is alone, it *does* lead somewhere: to a dark, magical world with a frightening "Other Mother" and "Other Father." Other Mother has curved, sharp fingernails and buttons for eyes. Other Father has buttons for eyes, too, and a long, pointy needle for sewing buttons into Coraline's eyes. Eventually, Coraline has to save her real parents from her Other parents—and escape herself.

Neil's *The Graveyard Book,* which was published in 2008, was inspired as he watched his two-year-old son ride his tricycle around a cemetery near the family home. Neil remembered reading Rudyard Kipling's *The Jungle Book,* about a boy raised by animals. Neil's hero in *The Graveyard Book* is raised by ghosts.

Neil started thinking about *The Ocean at the End of the Lane* after his mother told him that a nearby farm dated back one thousand years. Although the farm turned out not to be quite that old, it didn't matter to Neil.

The Ocean at the End of the Lane was named the British Book Awards' Book of the Year for 2013. *Coraline* won a Bram Stoker Award for Best Work for Young Readers in 2002. *American Gods* had won the Award for Best Novel in 2001. *The Graveyard Book* won the Newbery Medal for children's books in 2009.

Neil's books have sold millions of copies. *Coraline* was made into an animated movie in 2009. *Good Omens* became a TV series in 2019.

It all adds up to make Neil one of the most popular writers in the world today. But what if . . . Neil's parents hadn't given him that set of The Chronicles of Narnia for his seventh birthday? What if . . . Neil hadn't sat down on that bench in a train station and found the comic book that was left behind? What if . . . he didn't live in a house with a door that opened onto a brick wall?

Readers shudder to imagine what they might have missed out on.

JOE HILL

JOE HILL

When Joe Hill was nine years old, he decided what he wanted to do when he grew up. It was "to murder people in interesting ways and invent fascinating, unexpected monsters," he says.

He didn't actually want to kill people, of course. But the youngster's decision to make a macabre living came in 1981 when he was on the set of the horror movie *Creepshow*. In the film, Joe played a young boy named Billy who got in trouble with his father for reading a comic book called *Creepshow*. To get back at his dad, Billy created a voodoo doll that he stabbed with pins. It gave his dad unexplained pains wherever Billy poked the doll.

Joe spent about a week filming his role on *Creepshow*. There was no formal childcare on the set, so whenever he wasn't filming, Joe was left in the company of Tom Savini. He was the man in charge of the special makeup effects for the movie. Savini took care of Joe while painting scars on killers and building monsters. Savini enjoyed his work so much that Joe decided then and there that he wanted to get into the killing and monster business, too. And that's exactly what he did—just not quite in the same way as Savini. Instead of a makeup brush and paint, Joe's tools are a computer and a pen. He is a hugely successful writer of horror fiction who has authored four novels, several short-story collections, and many comic books.

That Joe is a big-time horror writer does not surprise his fans. Even Joe admits that it was "almost inevitable that I wound up writing ghost stories." After all, Joe is the son of Stephen and Tabitha King. Stephen is the best-selling horror author of all time and the man who wrote the movie *Creepshow*.

Tabitha is a successful author in her own right, with eight novels to her credit, as well as nonfiction titles, short stories, and poetry. "Everything I know about writing," Joe says, "I learned from my dad—if I didn't learn it from my mom first."

Joe is the middle child among Stephen and Tabitha's three kids. He has an older sister, Naomi, and a younger brother, Owen. Joe Hillström King was born in Bangor, Maine, in 1972. By the time Joe was six, Stephen was reading comic books such as *Bring on the Bad Guys* to him. *Bring on the Bad Guys* featured tales of Marvel's legendary superheroes like the Fantastic Four and Spider-Man, but young Joe's imagination was sparked more by the new villains it introduced. Doctor Doom, the Dread Dormammu, the Abomination, and more made their debuts: "grinning, lurid psychopaths who made unreasonable demands and bit their enemies in the face," Joe says. "I could relate to all of them because I was only about six years old, and I wanted to do all those things, too!"

He was ten when *Creepshow* first played in movie theaters. By that time, Joe's friends were starting to read magazines such as *Sports Illustrated* or *Rolling Stone*.

He was reading *Fangoria*, a magazine for fans of horror films. Later, while his friends were reading books by well-known fiction writers such as John Updike and Alice Munro, Joe was reading comics by Neil Gaiman and the great British comic book writer Alan Moore.

Joe was only thirteen when he started writing his own short stories. He went on to Vassar College in New York, where he earned a degree in English. At Vassar, he also came to an important decision: He wanted to write under the name Joe Hill. There were a couple of reasons for that. First, Joe did not want to have any publisher buy his work simply because he was Stephen King's son, neither to get close to Stephen nor to generate sales just because of the name. And second, Joe figured that if someone picked up a book that maybe wasn't all that great but got published just because of his name, they would never give him another chance.

Joe didn't tell anybody his true identity. His early fans didn't know. His editors didn't know. He even kept it a secret from his agent for eight years! But it took some time for writing as Joe Hill to produce results. It was ten years before his first book, a collection of short stories called *20th Century Ghosts*, came out in 2005. He also wrote four novels during that time but, he says, he was turned down by every publisher in New York, London, and even Canada.

In 2007, Joe made it to print with a novel for the first time. *Heart-Shaped Box* is about a rock star who collects spooky things. He gets more than he bargained for when he buys a dead man's suit off the Internet—with the ghost of the dead man still in it!

Once *Heart-Shaped Box* hit the shelves, it didn't take long for people to figure out that Joe Hill was Stephen King's son. After all, Joe looks exactly like Stephen did at an earlier age. Joe's mannerisms are much the same as his dad's, too. There was no way he could hide that from readers who got a glimpse of him on a book tour. At first, Joe considered having someone pretend to be him and do the book readings in his place. But he figured he wouldn't be able to keep the secret much longer, anyway. And by then he'd already been accepted as a writer who could stand on his own merits. *20th Century Ghosts* won several awards, including the Bram Stoker Award for Best Fiction Collection. *Heart-Shaped Box* went on to reach number eight on the *New York Times* best-seller list.

Three years later, Joe wrote *Horns,* a book about a man with demonic powers—and horns growing out of his head. It was made into a movie. Then in 2013, *NOS4A2* (pronounced "Nosferatu") hit number five on the best-seller list. *NOS4A2* might be Joe's scariest novel. The title is a tribute to Dracula, called Nosferatu in a 1922 horror film. However, instead of sucking human blood, Joe's vampire, Charlie Manx, drives a car that is powered by the souls of human children. That keeps him young even though he is 104.

In 2016, *The Fireman* became Joe's first number-one best seller. In *The Fireman,* a disease that causes humans to burst into flames is terrifying—but not as terrifying as the things people will do to save themselves. That is one of Joe's recurring themes: The way humans sometimes treat one another can be worse than any horrifying monster.

In 2019, Joe wrote a story for a new *Creepshow* series streaming on Netflix. The director for the installment, called "By the Silver Water of Lake Champlain," was Tom Savini—his old baby sitter on the *Creepshow* movie in the early 1980s. Because of the way things come full circle like that, Joe says, "Life sometimes really is like a novel." Or, putting it more like the writer of skin-crawling fiction that he is, "like a snake eating its tail."